GW01425252

Published by FUPE

Not a Playbook

art
The ~~science~~ of building a brand

Damian Bradfield and Andreas Tzortzis

QUALITIES

REFLECTION

Don't write
a playbook,

or a framework.

Don't write
a eulogy, either.

In 2016, we produced three beautiful, small books: Doubt, Time and Magic.

We asked a group of artists and contributors to write about whichever of the above themes most resonated with their creative process.

We were inundated with an incredible selection of work and submissions—from Hanna Hanra, Richard Curtis, Craig Mod, Douglas Coupland, Giles Duley and many others. However, the theme that resonated the most with me was doubt, which I struggle with daily.

Is my work good enough?
Will my work be appreciated?
Will the work stand out?
Will this make a difference?
Will anyone care?

As WeTransfer turns 15 and I enter a new chapter in my life, I wanted to document what we had achieved, to show (proudly) some of the incredible output of our studio and editorial team to an audience that often has no concept that we are anything other than a file-sharing business. And to remember and celebrate with those who have participated in this incredible journey.

But, as per usual, as my fingers touch
the keyboard or pen hovers above the notebook,
I focus immediately on the why?

Why would I imagine this would be unlike
any other project? Why was I thinking I'd just
knock this out in a month? Delusion. Oh, yes,
hello again, my old friend. The difference, however, was that 15 years on, it is now clear to
me that the reason for the level of doubt and
introspection is that we or I never wanted
the approval of the mainstream; we wanted
the approval of the artist—primarily from those
who hold the highest standards, that we knew
would hold us to the highest standards. We never
wanted to produce "Fast and Furious" block-
busters, god forbid, nor be Jeff Koons creating
blow-up dogs (keep it clean) or to be the Back-
street Boys.

We wanted to be seen by artists the way
they see David Lynch, David Bowie, Marlene
Dumas, Virginia Woolf, Thelonious Monk or
Martin Margiela—the artist's artist. Those who
don't conform, presumably do not have a playbook and dare to be different.

We had brand guidelines, but they were
just to maintain a look and feel. Most of the time,
we ignored them, pushed them and pulled them.
The company has repeatedly tried to install
the dreaded OKR into our work , but we've suc-
cessfully rejected it for nearly a decade now.

Our goal was to inspire, challenge and provoke, and we wanted to achieve the highest possible creative output with the means available to us.

Halfway through this book project, we canned it. (Hello doubt, long time no see.) We wanted to create an inspiring document, but to do so meant finding logic or perhaps even that dreaded word, a framework. "DUM DUM DUM!" It didn't seem to make sense, and it was becoming that f&*king thing I said I never wanted—a playbook.

So we took a step back, brought in Andreas, and went on a journey with him, uncovering rationale we didn't know existed. We interviewed artists and employees and considered this an investigation into what made WeTransfer different from his perspective, as opposed to mine or ours.

It's been challenging to rationalize our decision-making. You might feel that or read that at times during this exercise. It felt sometimes confrontational to see that it was often irrational, highly intuition-based and contradictory. But I cannot forget that, on many occasions, artists have asked us to talk more openly and be more transparent about our process to help them set a higher bar for other brands and enable artists to partner with brands on better terms.

I am proud that WeTransfer and WePresent have been respected, well-used, well-read and, dare I say it, even loved* by some of the world's leading artists.

At times, it would appear as if we were just lucky that some of the best in the world would reach out to us.

But I believe you must create luck; it doesn't land at your feet. Our team has produced some of the most inspirational work I have ever seen through a lot of hard work and, at times, considerable pushback.

This book is here for you, Elijah, Gilles, Alain, Russell, Riz, Marina, Davis, Malika** and everyone else who pushed us to share our secrets. Doing so has helped us better define what drove us and what a new process might look like elsewhere.

Why? So that others might take our creative baton and improve on what we started.

— Damian Bradfield,
co-founder of WeTransfer

---

*   Hearing Sir Peter Blake talk about how much he loved WeTransfer was a highlight :)
**   Elijah, Gilles Peterson, Alain de Botton, Russell Tovey, Riz Ahmed, Marina Abramović, Davis Guggenheim and Malika Favre.

+ Add files

Transfer

wetransfer

THE SUN CHASES + SCAT
IT SCATTERS RED LIGHT>> T
WHEN WE ARE CLOUDLESS
THE SCREENS WHICH CIRC
// ALL YOUR TOMORROWS
FALLS. DIGITAL CULTURE CR
TREMOR/ DIGITAL CULTURE
UNCONSCIOUS HIPSTER C
GLAMOUR FROM THE YAC
RE-INHABIT THE CENTRE /
SAVED FROM THE HEART C

DEARDTLA.COM

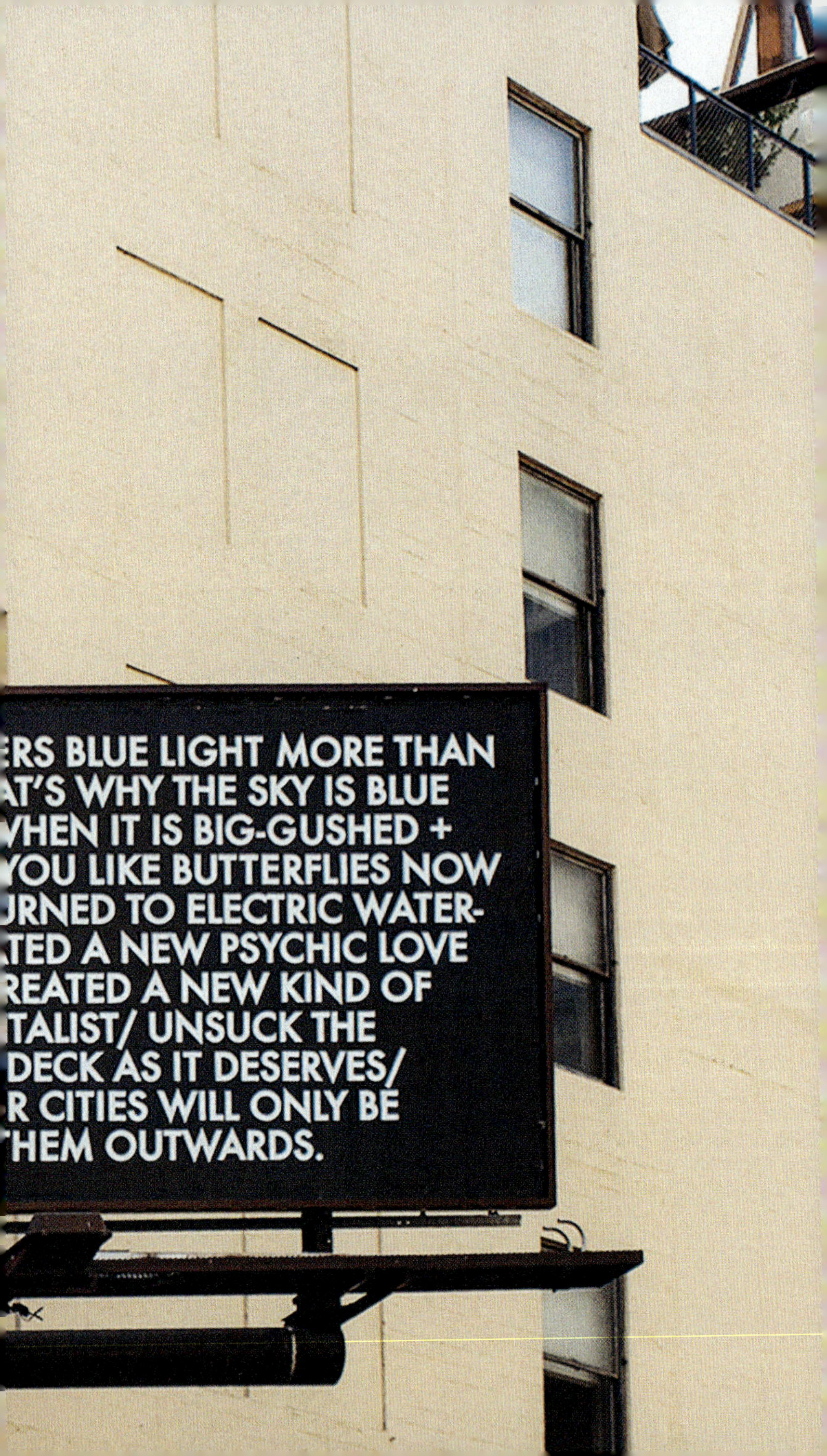

ERS BLUE LIGHT MORE THAN
AT'S WHY THE SKY IS BLUE
WHEN IT IS BIG-GUSHED +
YOU LIKE BUTTERFLIES NOW
URNED TO ELECTRIC WATER-
TED A NEW PSYCHIC LOVE
REATED A NEW KIND OF
TALIST/ UNSUCK THE
DECK AS IT DESERVES/
R CITIES WILL ONLY BE
THEM OUTWARDS.

1.	Penguin Books
Fans of the storied British
publisher, the WeTransfer
team asked if they could
feature Penguin's latest
releases on any unsold
wallpaper inventory. When
Penguin sent them portrait
images in the wrong format,
WeTransfer's bare bones
creative team restaged and
reshot them. The gesture
earned the brand a collaboration with actor and author
Sir Stephen Fry.

2.	John Legend
An image from the "Can't
Just Preach" video series
WePresent collaborated
on with John Legend,
about activists turning talk
into change.

3.	Gem Fletcher
	and Ken Hermann
An image from "The Well of
Death," a story by creative
director Gem Fletcher and
photographer Ken Hermann
on India's high-octane
stuntman tradition, featured
on WePresent.

4.	Catherine Hyland
The British photographer
captured young Mongolian
sumo wrestlers for WePre-
sent in her series "The Rise
of the Mongolians."

5.	Mr. Wash
"Emancipation Procla-
mation," shown here, was
painted by Fulton Leroy
Washington, a.k.a. Mr. Wash,
while serving a life sen-
tence for a non-violent drug
offense. Upon his pardon by
President Barack Obama,
WeTransfer commissioned
a documentary on the artist
and the practice he developed behind bars.

6.	Björk
WeTransfer helped fund
Björk's music video for
the song "Arisen My
Senses," which featured
giant slug-like creatures
designed by Jesse Kanda.
Pictured above are behind-
the-scenes images from
the shoot.

7.	Dear DTLA
Between 2015 and 2016,
the Ace Hotel and WeTransfer
invited a different artist each
month to take over the billboard outside the hotel in
downtown LA. This image
shows one designed by
London-based text artist and
poet Robert Montgomery.

LONGEVITY

Build a tech
company

by refusing to
act like one.

Then grow
a brand.

The email from the actor's manager sat in the inbox of WePresent's outgoing editor for a few days. As one of his last acts before he left the company, he forwarded it to the new editor of WeTransfer's arts platform.

She wrote back, and within a few months got a treatment for a politically-provocative short film the actor was desperate to shoot. It was going to be a very personal project, one that captured his thoughts and fears as a South Asian Briton living in the UK after Brexit. They were looking for financing and distribution. The two people privy to the email chain at WeTransfer said yes, instinctively.

A little over two years later, they were in LA, sitting in The Dolby Theatre, watching as Riz Ahmed and director Aneil Karia won the 2022 Oscar for Best Live Action Short Film for their film, "The Long Goodbye."

They did not expect this. To be honest, nobody did.

You might never have heard of WeTransfer until now. Maybe you're aware of the file-sharing service, but I am willing to bet all of the stolen bikes in Holland that 99.9 percent of you have never heard the story we're going to share. Because if you had, then you would know that the path from a converted canal-side house in Amsterdam to The Dolby Theatre isn't that winding after all.

And while the book's title is a bit of a joke, it also aims to shine a light on the culture and strategy that enabled a functional file-sharing service from the Netherlands to build a global brand as a platform and patron of the creative community. It did so while profitably growing year-on-year, and donating millions to support its audience.

That culture and strategy was built on trustworthy intentions, recast the way a brand should work with artists, and—crucially—formed itself around people who thought similarly about a tech company's potential to set forth powerful, creative ideas into the world.

There was also a good amount of delusion. But successful brands are often built by people who are delusional—who don't believe that A should connect to B, but to the rings of Saturn, instead.

WeTransfer had people like this and, in building the company, they borrowed from the best qualities of the very creatives they served: intention, trust, faith and instinct, with no small amount of serendipity sprinkled in.

Now feels like the right time to talk about this, and not just because your bookshelf was looking a little thin. For one, it seems as if our collective horizon has shrunk. We know that it typically takes years to build a brand. Yet the expectation now is that you can MrBeast anything if you can throw enough paid ad dollars at YouTube. And you have to, because the average CMO has a lifespan of three years, so the focus is on the short term.

This book is here to show the value in developing for the long term.

Second, brands are valuable only insofar as they maintain an internal culture and belief system that can outlive the people working there. That culture and those people need to feel as if they're pushing for a bigger vision beyond revenue goals.

This book aims to show you the importance of starting with one.

Third, the boardroom is skewed toward the analyst, especially now that we have access to so much data. Brands are products, and customers are users, meant to be converted then chased again, whether they need to buy or not. This approach suggests that a brand can be built by a predictive logic.

This book argues the opposite.

Before we start, some housekeeping.

There's an issue with the word "brand." Much like "content," it's been pulled and stretched to accommodate contexts that have muddled its definition.

So for the purposes of this book, when you see me (more on that below) referring to a "brand," I mean a company that holds a place in your head because it's worked hard to connect you to its products or message.

More than a logo, name or a visual identity (which, in the age of generative AI, can be spun up in minutes) we're talking about successful companies that build an emotional connection with their customer base over time. They accomplish this by being intentional, trustworthy and not afraid to push boundaries in how they tell their story, and with whom they collaborate.

This is important to establish right from the jump, as today the belief is that any company that launches with a logo and has something to sell is by default a brand.

This book argues differently.

So here's a company that, on the strength of a single product built 15 years ago, reaches 80 million monthly active users and more than 600,000 paying subscribers in 190 countries. As of printing, WeTransfer has reported year-on-year growth and profitability for the past decade, and more than €100 million in annual revenue[1]. It's also a brand that has commissioned thousands of creative projects, and worked with some of the world's most influential artists. Through its innovative wallpaper strategy, it has given away billions of home page ad impressions to artists and arts nonprofits. And through its Supporting Act Foundation, which started in 2021, it has given away more than €1 million a year in unconditional grants, with an ambition to impact 1,000,000 emerging artists by 2035.

It is a brand that won an Oscar not because of a campaign, but because of the sum of all of those things.

But very few people seem to know about it.

So I was asked to write about it. And with a background in journalism and years in narrative strategy in the brand world, I approached it the way I might any new brief: I looked at the work WeTransfer created over the last 15 years, and talked to the people that helped imagine it and put it out in the world.

What follows over the next hundred or so pages is my attempt to put down in writing the methods, moments and culture that helped make WeTransfer a global brand. There are also lots of pretty pictures and recaps of some of the brand's best work.

There's a bit of delusion in all of this as well, of course, because the first rule of the WeTransfer Playbook is that there is no playbook.

There are values though. And those values led to specific actions.

Those actions drove WeTransfer to a position not as a prominent brand, but a loved one—a brand that managed to turn its user base into an actual community that thought of the platform as a partner, and a champion.

The team did it—often to their detriment—not by commanding attention, but by resonating with the people they most wanted to reach. So let's call them a lower case b brand. REI, not North Face. John Malkovich, not Dwayne Johnson. And here's what defines them:

They walk before
they run.

        They bring their audi-
        ence along with them.

                They believe values
                are useful only when
                they lead to action.

I've defined the actions they took at the top of each chapter.

These didn't exist at the beginning of this project, but were developed in the five months we interviewed people at the brand and dived into the work they put out into the world.

That's important context to anyone reading this who wants to borrow from the WeTransfer approach. These actions weren't points on an internal presentation, but a lived ethos that fed a brand personality so singular, it had its own instincts and reflexes.

It was these actions that helped shape the WeTransfer personality and turn it into a loved brand.

For you? They might guide the way you think about building a company culture. They might change the way you work with artists. Or maybe they just make you think differently about the way brands reach us, inspire us and the role they play in our lives.

INTENTION

Don't build for
a customer base.

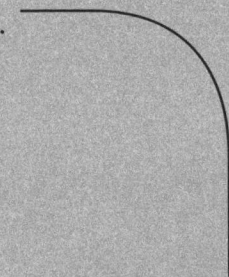

Build for a community, with
an intention beyond profitability.

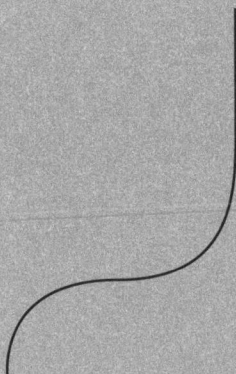

That narrative differentiates
a brand and makes it relevant.

The late British academic Sir Ken Robinson's charming, seemingly off-the-cuff TED talk, "Do Schools Kill Creativity?" has been viewed more than 78 million times on the TED channel (at the time of printing). A childhood polio survivor, the esteemed educationalist had made a name for himself with bold ideas on education reform since the 1990s. But it was TED in 2006—then in its infancy—that introduced him to a wider audience. It's the most viewed talk in the organization's history, and it's been translated into 62 languages.

By the time he entered WeTransfer's orbit ten years later, he had published "Finding Your Element," which included the concept of Flow, a theory pioneered by Hungarian-American psychologist Mihaly Robert Csikszentmihalyi.

WeTransfer met Robinson in 2016 in a dimly-lit breakfast room in a London hotel and the two sides hit it off. Over the next few months, he would describe for WeTransfer's founders what they intrinsically felt but had never articulated: their product, with its lack of distraction and demands for sign-ups, worked to keep creatives in their Flow.

You know Flow. That state where you lose awareness of where you are as your mind grooves into a sustained period of focus. It's hard to attain, and easy to lose. The positioning was as simple as the design of the file-sharing service, which came out of a frustration with the status quo.

Back in 2009, when WeTransfer first launched, file-sharing was dominated by companies like Yousendit, Rapid Share and Mega Upload. Most had a seedy vibe, often serving as a hub for piracy and pornography. Upload speeds were regularly throttled in order to push subscription plans for faster service. The sites themselves represented the very worst of web 2.0 design: cluttered, with cheesy typefaces, bad colors and irrelevant banner ads. The platforms were designed for ensnarement, not experience.

So the founders of WeTransfer decided to do something about it. Into a landscape dominated by engineers and the supremacy of the code base, they entered with little more than a clearly-defined aesthetic sensibility.

Their approach:
people first,
creativity second,
technology third.

"People first" meant finding great people, and leading them with empathy and trust. Second, those people should be empowered to be as creative as possible in building the product.

A positioning as simple as the design of the site.

"Technology third" meant designing a plat-form that didn't dig its elbows into the first two priorities, like someone forcing their way into a conversation.

> Great technology would be
> a product of great people,
> empowered.

And so, on December 5, 2009, WeTransfer launched with a simple, friendly flash site that had little more than a few lines of copy and some buttons. The users came quickly and suddenly, arriving via word-of-mouth and the personalized recommendation engine StumbleUpon (RIP). Within three months, people in 187 countries were using WeTransfer. Within three years, they had 15 million monthly users.

But there were still questions about its via-bility as a business, especially from the potential venture capital investors the founders had begun courting in 2014. They had an advertising format that didn't adhere to industry standard and very limited data to share with potential advertisers. Plus, of course, at this time Google was "eating everyone's lunch." (They heard this sentence over and over again from 2010 to 2024.)

They had traveled to London and Silicon Valley with dreams of becoming the owners of a unicorn. They were seduced by the idea of belonging to an exclusive club, looking for acceptance and perhaps acknowledgement that they, too, had created something special.

But their narrative was off.

They were a bunch of guys with design and media backgrounds set up in a house on the Nieuwe Prinsengracht in Amsterdam, with a strangely simple product that left all sorts of revenue opportunities on the table.

Investors saw the year-on-year growth that by 2013 had made the company profitable for the first time, thanks to steady advertising and subscriber growth. But they were puzzled as to why WeTransfer wouldn't make their piece of real estate even more valuable.

They could add more advertising space to it, for example, or make it easier to sell ads by conforming to industry standards, or introduce a sign-up that yielded them customer information that could be used for targeting or sold to third-party vendors.

> For the founders, who had built a technological safe haven that protected its users' privacy and process, none of this made any sense.

Why would they change WeTransfer to something that directly contradicted the values they held?

They ended this period in 2014, empty-handed but resolved. The 15 million users on WeTransfer every month were proof that their nonconformist approach was working.

They kept their day jobs and continued selling full-screen ads—they called them wallpapers—on their platform. They went door-to-door in London, and tried the same in Paris, offering the digital equivalent of the double-page ads for luxury brands found in fashion magazines to this day.

If they were hoping the format would resonate, their timing was crap. Quick-hitting banner ads that targeted users based on their data was what excited media buyers and execs alike.

The result: a lot of unsold ad inventory. To make up for the loss they decided to showcase artists and arts organizations at scale. WeTransfer's design was intended to be free of distraction, but did it have to be free of inspiration?

It was a revelatory decision, even if in retrospect it seems hard for them to pinpoint the moment it happened. That's a shame, because it might have given me a better way to start the book.

Still, a move like that isn't made randomly. The reason Patagonia began making its popular Synchilla jackets from recycled plastic soda bottles in 1993 was that the company culture—founded with a commitment to the out-

"Blackalachia"
with Moses Sumney

Sumney originally conceived "Blackalachia" as a live album combining songs from his albums "Aromanticism" and "Græ." When the pandemic scrapped those plans, he turned to WeTransfer with the hope of creating a concert film instead. Shot over two days in the Blue Ridge Mountains near Asheville, North Carolina, the hour-long film, released in 2022, upended traditional live concert films and is the kind of project that might not have seen the light of day without the brand's help.

doors—demanded every measure that reduced environmental impact[2].

WeTransfer's founders, similarly, had come from the art and design world. One had made his name with a successful design blog, one had launched a creative platform and the third a creative agency. They had a deep appreciation for the creative process and reverence for the artists that made great work.

> Highlighting those artists felt like the beginning of a conversation with the hundreds of thousands of creatives that had begun using WeTransfer.

And that's the best a brand can hope for, really: The opportunity to have a conversation with people.

AirBnB—launched in August 2008, just a little over a year before WeTransfer—felt much like this at the beginning. In a hospitality marketplace dominated by hotel chains and a confusing mix of vacation rental agencies, AirBnB offered a simple, human solution. The digital tool was an easy way to book a place to stay, but its intention was to connect people—guests and hosts—in a more meaningful way.

As a result, it stood out from so many of its startup contemporaries. The tool didn't just address a need, but did so with an intention beyond simply market fit. That made it easier to build a brand that promised a unique human experience around what was essentially a well-designed booking marketplace.

AirBnB differentiated itself and grew into a global brand on the back of this narrative; its storytelling focused on the community of users that booked and hosted.

Building with an intention beyond profit smoothes the way to building a brand, because it makes it easier for your customers to form an emotional connection to you.

> In using its digital real estate to showcase artists—first 50 percent of the yearly inventory, eventually 30 percent as ad sales picked up—WeTransfer didn't just signal authenticity, it reflected and celebrated the creatives that used it.

The effect on the brand was that WeTransfer—much like Apple—became code for working in the creative industry. If you used the product, chances are you were a filmmaker, photographer, musician, designer, illustrator or creative who needed to send large files.

And creatives tend to identify closely with the brands they use, and assign greater meaning

A design free of distraction,

not free of inspiration.

to them. That connection has not just helped
WeTransfer to grow the product to meet different
demands and anticipate new ones, it has also
helped them shape a brand personality.

MUSICIAN AND FILMMAKER
MOSES SUMNEY ON INTENTION

Tell us about how intentional you are in creating something.

It's important to have conviction in the creative process, because you as the artist have to be the first fan of the idea. You can't expect other people to believe in it and support it if you don't fully believe in it and support it. And you're going to have so many naysayers and obstacles that come up in the process of creating that idea that you will need the conviction to overcome it. The most important thing for a piece of contemporary art to do is to have a point of view, and to have a perspective on the self and the world that is unique to the vision of the artist. And you need conviction in order to stay true to the vision, and in order to establish a voice that is unique to the art itself.

56

You typically have a lot of collaborators, how do you ensure they approach the work with your same intention?

As someone who is questioning the world as it is presented to us constantly in my art, I try to pick creative collaborators who approach their world with a similar type of vision. That way I'm not fighting an uphill battle trying to convince people who don't even see the world in the same way that I do. Or don't even see the world with curiosity. It's not like I need everyone to think the same. It's better if we disagree on some things, but I need to know they're at least curious about expanding their world view. And then I try to pick collaborators that already fuck with me, to be honest.

TRUST

Influencers and creators bring their
je ne sais quoi and audience to a brand.

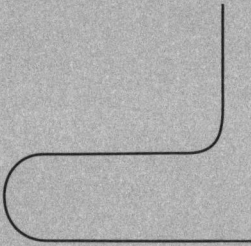

Don't try to buy
their trust.

Enable them creatively,
and earn it.

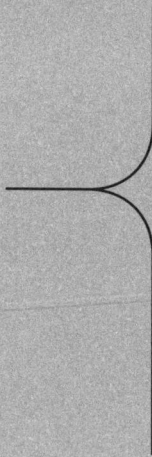

Authenticity
follows.

You may have forgotten this, given the prevalence of always-on streaming, but there was a period during which new music was released via MP3. And though WeTransfer was aware of studios using the service to send files back and forth, the revelation that musicians used it to drop exclusive tracks came a few years into its existence—thanks to one particularly prominent one.

On November 18, 2013, Prince released a new track, "Da Bourgeois," via a WeTransfer link. The move throttled the Dutch company's servers as an avalanche of Prince fans hovered their cursors over it and clicked. The team was delighted of course, but also flummoxed. And WeTransfer got no answers, because Paisley Park didn't return emails.

Two years later, Prince appeared again, after asking his concert promoter, AEG Live, to release the album he produced for singer Judith Hill via WeTransfer, and blast the link to the entirety of its email database. The move had a similar effect on the platform's servers, now a bit more robust.

The buzz was enough for WeTransfer to hire someone to begin building relationships within the music industry, to see how the company might work better with artists.

Between 2013 and 2017, Bon Iver, Twenty One Pilots, Woodkid, Azealia Banks, Oasis, Moby, Leon Bridges, De La Soul, Bonobo and others used WeTransfer to release music directly to their fans. The brand was able to show musicians that their audiences would respond positively to the notion of a "gift" from them, a one-off present from the artist to the fan—with no catch.

It was through that work that the brand connected with FKA twigs, whose manager sent an email to the team in the summer of 2016 with an idea for a project.

The British dancer and singer was touring her debut album, "LP1," through the US. She'd fallen in love with the city of Baltimore, which at the time was grappling with the death of Freddie Gray at the hands of police officers. Her intent was to showcase a different side of the hardscrabble city, one that celebrated its individuality and creativity.

On Twitter, she announced a dance workshop, the day before her concert, for anyone who loved dance and wanted to show up. She planned to film it, and asked the WeTransfer team if the brand would finance and host it.

The company had contributed money to projects before. Those requests tended to come in from friends who were artists. It also commissioned photographers and funded the occasional music video. But this marked the first time it would create something together with an artist, a project it could release exclusively.

There were no well-crafted decks circulating among the C-suite for months ahead of the project, and no KPIs assigned to it. There was no existing product campaign it could fit into, and twigs wasn't a paid ambassador for the brand.

> There was just a sense that this was a meaningful project for WeTransfer to throw its weight behind and a worthwhile artist to build with, and there was trust that her team would pull it off at a high level.

The result, "Baltimore Dance Project," proved a milestone in WeTransfer's relationship with creative collaborators.

It was the beginning of a new era of story-telling for the brand: increased budgets, bigger artists but also more real-time decision-making and guerrilla-style marketing.

The project was the boldest—and to that point most expensive—example of the brand prioritizing creative authenticity over deliberate marketing outcomes. But its foundations had been laid earlier.

I've talked about the wallpaper, but what I didn't mention is that the artists featured on it in the early days had no idea what was coming until their websites crashed from all the extra traffic. Keep it mind, this was a different era: Squarespace or Mailchimp weren't around or prominent enough to offer their one-shop solution for website creation, marketing and email management.

Artists were way out of their depth. WeTransfer often received annoyed emails from them, asking who was going to pay for the extra server costs to get their websites up and running again.

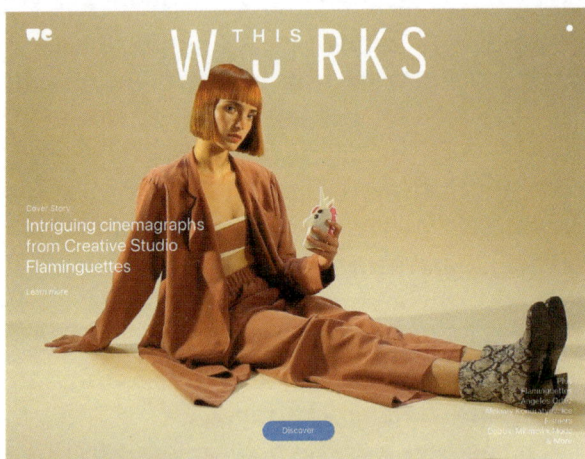

This Works celebrated artists and creatives, many from the WeTransfer community.

The company answered their gripes with an editorial platform that did a better job of highlighting their work. They called it This Works.

After clicking the wallpaper image, WeTransfer directed the user to This Works to read stories about the photographers, illustra-

Where Prince goes, others follow.

WeTransfer's film with FKA twigs was a simple, joyous documentation of artist and fans celebrating a common passion.

tors, filmmakers and other creatives featured, many of whom used the product.

This was a common strategy at the time. Borrowing from media and publishing, brands like Red Bull had built content platforms and hired editorial teams, assigning them the task of defining and telling stories around the "playgrounds" that would build brand awareness with new audiences. Those teams rarely saw themselves as marketers, and believed the best way to build connection with an audience was through instinct and awareness of the cultural landscape.

This Works hired editors from the art and journalism worlds who brought their own connections and creative ideas.

The storytelling platform, renamed WePresent in 2018, became an emissary for the brand. WePresent's eclectic editorial philosophy—held together under the broad strapline "Unexpected stories of creativity"—allowed the team freedom in the subjects and creatives they featured.

> The idea was to offer the same moments of surprise and delight you'd get walking through a museum.

At the time of writing, the site and associated social media still get 3 million monthly visits from an audience that's able to peruse anything from

An arts platform for inspiration, and context.

manifestos by artists, such as photographer Martin Parr, to articles on the boon menstrual cycles can be to women's creativity (2019's most popular piece), or immerse themselves in interactive microsites, like Seb Emina's charming Wild Memory Radio.

The beauty of WePresent remains its inquisitive, gamboling editorial strategy. All content platforms eventually find themselves succumbing to traffic-generating topics and formats. WePresent—with its stories on Tehranian sound artists, a record label hailing from a Cameroonian jail or professional namers in Northern California — never seemed to have this problem.

Since 2018, annual guest curators—including performance artist Marina Abramović, singer/songwriter Solange Knowles, actor Russell Tovey and, in 2024, conceptual artist Olafur Eliasson—have elevated new talents to prominence on WePresent, and used their year-long residency to put forth creative projects into the world.

WePresent rarely talks about the WeTransfer product (the two also don't share the same visual language). Rather, the platform—and its social handles, email newsletters and events—serves as another way to engage with a user base that might not need to send large files all that frequently.

The stories would inspire making. Making would result in large files that needed trans-

ferring. WeTransfer, through
WePresent, would stay top of
mind in that process.

But the platform's position in the brand world is
increasingly rare.

In the early 2020s, Meta, TikTok, Google's
YouTube, and to some degree Search, became
the main storytelling channels available to
brands. Every company that hopes to stay top of
mind to its customer base, or tell bigger stories
beyond its products, are still beholden to the pay-
to-play policies and shifting algorithms of those
cynically-run behemoths.

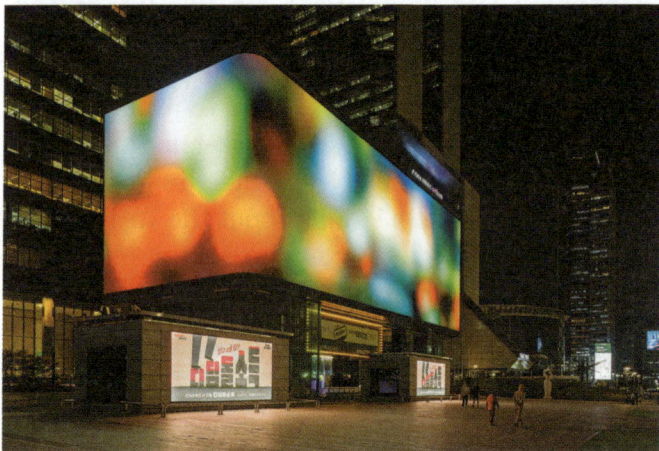

A collaboration between Eliasson, WeTransfer and the public art
organization CIRCA, "Lifeworld" took over billboards in four major
intersections in the autumn of 2024 (K-Pop Square in Seoul, above).

To stick out, brands are reliant on hyper-active, often unhinged, social handles, whose success is measured by how well they mimic prevailing trends and create stunt content rather than communicate larger brand ideas. Witness the language app Duolingo, which has a TikTok handle that has absolutely dominated the early 2020s with posts that include members of its social team dressing in oversized owl costumes to wreak havoc on streets in cities around the world.

Entertaining? Absolutely. Furthering a brand purpose that promises the "best way to learn a language"? Not so much.

There is also a shifting of power, a growing tension between brand personality and creator personality.

Collaborations that do well are ones where the creator has primacy because of the power inherent in their hard-won audience—the very one that the brand covets.

As a result, it becomes harder for a brand to create the sort of universe that surprises and engages its audience with unexpected collaborations and quality storytelling.

And this universe is important. It creates context for products that are often hard to contextualize. Like file-sharing.

By the way, if you talk to some of the people who've been around WeTransfer from the beginning, they often lament the fact that they didn't have a physical product that people could hold and touch. That kind of product would've enabled the brand to create IRL experiences for its user base: opportunities for them to interact with the brand and one another.

Instead, they invested in digital experiences on their owned channels—This Works (later, WePresent) and the WeTransfer wallpaper. Those provide safe spaces for their collaborators, and promise more freedom in the creative execution.

Beginning with FKA twigs, This Works evolved from profiling artists to creating exclusive projects together with them. Often, that meant meeting artists in their liminal spaces, rather than showcasing the work that made them famous.

Russell Tovey, for example, has an impressive run of film and stage roles to his name and a popular art podcast. But during his guest curatorship of WePresent, he wanted to make a documentary on the 1980s artist David Robilliard, as part of his focus on highlighting artists lost too young to the AIDS epidemic. So for months, WePresent dedicated a small team to work on the production with Tovey and produce a microsite. They also organized a live performance titled "BLUE NOW" that honored Derek Jarman's influential film, "Blue," about the epidemic.

"The Abramović Method" with Marina Abramović

Abramović served as guest curator of WePresent from 2020 to 2021. In addition to highlighting five-up-and-coming artists on the arts platform, she worked with WeTransfer's studio to create a microsite that would bring her lauded Abramović Method (until then limited to live performances) online.

The interactive site featured her exercises aimed at enhancing concentration and mindfulness. She wrapped up the partnership with an exhibition at the Old Truman Brewery in London. Following the collaboration, Abramović became a WeTransfer advocate, recommending other artists to the platform.

Artists, musicians and creatives are some of the most desirable ambassadors for brands, which want both their authenticity and their followings. For this, companies are willing to pay a lot of money—and this is where the artists' leverage often shifts dramatically. With every contract between an artist and a brand, there are guidelines the artist must observe in creating for that company. Logo placement, yes, but also subjects to avoid, messages to emphasize, and so on.

WeTransfer rarely had such agreements in place, beyond the bare minimum. Until recently, it didn't retain the rights to any of the artists' work for the brand. (The company now shares IP on some films it has co-produced.)

And the permission the team gave artists to do the work was broad. Astonishingly broad, in fact, given the size of the brand. In the conversations I had with WeTransfer veterans who steered these partnerships, not one copped to submitting a set of brand guidelines or conditions to an artist, a detail they served up with no small amount of delight.

Forget incorporating the product or a clever line of copy. Most of the time, they left the logo out of the collaboration entirely, much to the annoyance of the PR and comms team.

But this was as intentional as the design of the product itself. WeTransfer knew its community

valued the brand for its sub-
tlety. By ceding the spotlight
to the artist, it connected even
more to that audience.

WeTransfer booked the billboard outside of the Ace Hotel
in DTLA for nine months in 2015, featuring a new artist every
month. The WeTransfer logo was nowhere to be found on
the work itself.

If it felt too slick, or like too much of a transaction,
then the projects landed poorly. WeTransfer's
success with these collaborations depended
on an artist feeling passionate about the work
they did, and the team believed that the more
involved the brand became, the greater the risk
to the quality of the work.

WePresent worked closely with the artists
in bringing their projects to life; it also made sure
to protect the creative process from anything

Trust that benefits the artist,

and sends a signal.

that felt like overt marketing. Often, though it provided the platform and budget, WeTransfer had very little left over for paid advertising to promote the work.

That's probably why you didn't know that the brand commissioned a video for Björk, produced Little Simz's first narrative short film or released a visual album with jazz supernova Kamasi Washington that featured in the Whitney Biennial.

The goal was never to monetize artists, but to create a meaningful, long-term relationship, perhaps even a friendship. And, yes, written down that reads a little bit naïve.

> You could make the argument that in choosing a light brand touch, WeTransfer missed out on reaching a bigger audience for the product.

But there's a tightrope that anyone who does this work at a brand must walk: doing right by the artist, and doing right by the company. Most often, the company wins out in that equation. But when the artist does, you tend to have the type of collaborations that yield if not a bigger then a more authentic outcome with their audiences, sometimes at a fraction of the price.

For artists, trust can feel like a solitary endeavor. Most trust in their talent, and that

the effort they put into something will yield
a work of which they can be proud. Rarely, do
they receive it from a brand collaboration.

For a brand, this is the long game of small
bets. And it's a hard concept to sell through, even
though every one of them craves authenticity. It
takes time, which, in this day and age, is a com-
modity in short supply.

Filmed over two days, "Baltimore Dance
Project" told a story of connection, movement and joy around the gathering of almost
400 people who showed up to the workshop.
The brand provided an exclusive trailer to
The Baltimore Sun website that directed people
to the film on This Works.

In addition to the video, WeTransfer also
created a microsite. And though there might have
been no KPIs, the newly hired comms manager
worked the media and music blog circuit hard,
netting a wide number of mentions.

Her only comment? The microsite didn't
have the WeTransfer logo anywhere on it.

PERFORMER FKA TWIGS
ON TRUST

How do you think brands should treat their artistic partners?

I know that, in my experience, when I have been trusted to create something original without control or without too many eyes spying on me, it's always been incredibly successful. Not only has it created a huge cultural impact but also reached a lot more people, numbers-wise, than when I've been coerced into fitting to a certain brief to sell something or to create an image that the brand is trying to convey.

How has trust benefited your work?

I think that in any relation-ship trust builds confidence, and a confident artist is going to make amazing work. I know that when a brand has believed in me, it's really helped me spread my wings to fly. I think that artists are often fragile creatures at the core of it all. When someone believes in us, it provides a support and provides the structure and the encouragement that we need to create something truly beautiful.

What is the role of each side?

There is a big difference between an artist and a creative, and I think brands are full of creatives who are integral to artists to help finish the vision and package the vision. But there's nothing like an artist's word, or world. Artists are original thinkers, and it's those original thoughts that capture the attention of the world. I think brands should trust their artistic collaborators because they're there to change the cultural DNA, they're there to think of something new, they're there to portray a message that no one has thought of before. There can be a really important and integral synergy between the house and the structure that a brand has managed to build and the artists' colors and paints that can fit within that frame.

83

FAITH

Create a culture
that rewards
passion...

... and ideas
that start

from
somewhere
else.

Then place faith in
people, not outcomes.

The members that make up the neo-soul and
R&B supergroup SAULT have never been
confirmed. There are strong suspicions, and
anyone at their concert in London in the winter
of 2023, could recognize their voices and styles
even through balaclavas and screens.

They maintain this level of mystery in all
facets. Albums—so far 11 in all—are released suddenly, and never via a streaming service. Major
record labels? There are none involved. They sub-
vert not just the platforms commonly used, but
the necessity of an always-on dialogue with fans.

And it makes them kind of a nightmare to
work with.

WeTransfer had—through no initiative of
its own—become the group's preferred distribution method from the beginning. The links would
be available only for a limited amount of time.
In November 2022, three years after their first
album, the group provided a download link for
five new albums, and sent fans on an Easter egg
hunt to try and find the password to unlock them.

That stunt raised alarms with WeTransfer's
cybersecurity team, who were convinced that
the sudden influx of people was a classic Distrib-
uted Denial of Service attack, where hackers
flood servers with traffic. SAULT, of course, hadn't
bothered to let them know, nor had any idea
that their treasure hunt could cause this big
a problem.

Take risks with brand, not product.

SAULT's members have never been definitely
confirmed, but their preference for distributing
music via WeTransfer has.

A year later, the group's producer, Inflo, and
WeTransfer reached a formal-ish agreement.
SAULT asked for a budget in the upper six
figures to help them create a visual album that
would be recorded at The British Museum. In
exchange, they offered WeTransfer exclusivity in
hosting the film that would give fans their first
peek behind the curtain of the elusive collective.
The brand agreed, without almost any conditions.
SAULT acknowledged WeTransfer's unique

patronage by titling the album, "Acts of Faith."
Faith is as good a word as any when it comes to
talking about a quality the best artists and brands
have. But there is nuance in the interpretation of it.

>An artist's faith is in the belief
>that the difficulty of the creative
>process will yield an idea they
>can be proud to share.

>A brand's faith is in believing
>that a culture that encourages
>bold ideas is worthwhile, even
>when the desired outcomes
>fall short.

For the past couple of chapters, you've read
about the unique level of trust WeTransfer
places in artists. It doesn't have big budgets, but
it invests in the projects of artists that reflect
its curious, ambitious brand personality. Those
artists want to repay that faith with work they
feel elevates the cultural discourse, and show up
in unpredictable ways.

With that approach comes more than a few
projects that fail to live up to their potential: a less-
than-expected collaboration with John Legend,
or campaigns around net neutrality and a NASA
anniversary that didn't hit the mark, or that hit
budget limits before they could truly resonate.

But they didn't bankrupt the company. Because there's a difference between taking risks with product, and taking risks with brand.

For a large part of its history, WeTransfer's product team was a small one. New features and updates required careful alignment to maximize the resources at hand. It's probably the reason that—though the team has launched additional creative apps and sharing tools—there hasn't been much change to the product since its inception.

But the other reason is that it works. It has a design aesthetic and personality loved by the customer base. Should WeTransfer tweak the product too much, it would risk losing its audience.

Weak collaborations and creative projects don't quite have that level of risk. If anything, they're worth a chance because of the potential that beckons from the other side: more brand awareness, equity and a chance to hold space in people's minds.

Those chances were becoming more important to WeTransfer in the mid-2010s as it matured out of its bootstrapping era. File-sharing and collaboration had become a very competitive space.

Google had popular collaboration tools, such as Drive and Docs, and Dropbox reigned supreme in the US. People were beginning to share files through Skype (which Microsoft had acquired in 2011) and even WhatsApp. Consumers made

choices based on speed, reliability and price.
Had WeTransfer listened purely to its marketing
research and focused its messaging on price, it
might have found itself in a race to the bottom
with competitors who could afford to wait it out.

For comparison, look at Uber and Lyft. They
had distinct brand personalities at the beginning:
Uber, the private black car that made everyone
feel like a VIP; Lyft, the mustachioed, friendlier
alternative that promised human connection.
Do you feel the same way about them now? Or do
you just choose the cheaper option that'll show
up quickest?

Lyft had managed to differentiate its story
in the marketplace, but as its product and service
regressed to the mean, that story was little more
than a hollow marketing play.

> WeTransfer's founders chose to
> invest in brand-building as a way
> to differentiate themselves and
> maintain the conversation with
> their audience, and the broader
> culture. But it could only work
> because their product teams
> upheld their end of the narrative.

They soon got confirmation from the investment
world for this approach. In 2015, they agreed to
outside investment for the first time: $25 million

"The Bunt Machine"
with Mac Premo

Man wanting to create a bizarre machine that bunts a baseball meets a brand keen to position itself as a trusted tool in the creative process. The result: a 2 minute and 30 second ad of a construction project, turned written play, turned one-man show that earned millions of views and award considerations in 2018. The original idea wasn't much clearer than those previous sentences, but WeTransfer trusted Premo, a commercials director, to deliver. In the process, the ad proved a good example of how WeTransfer might elegantly integrate its product into campaigns.

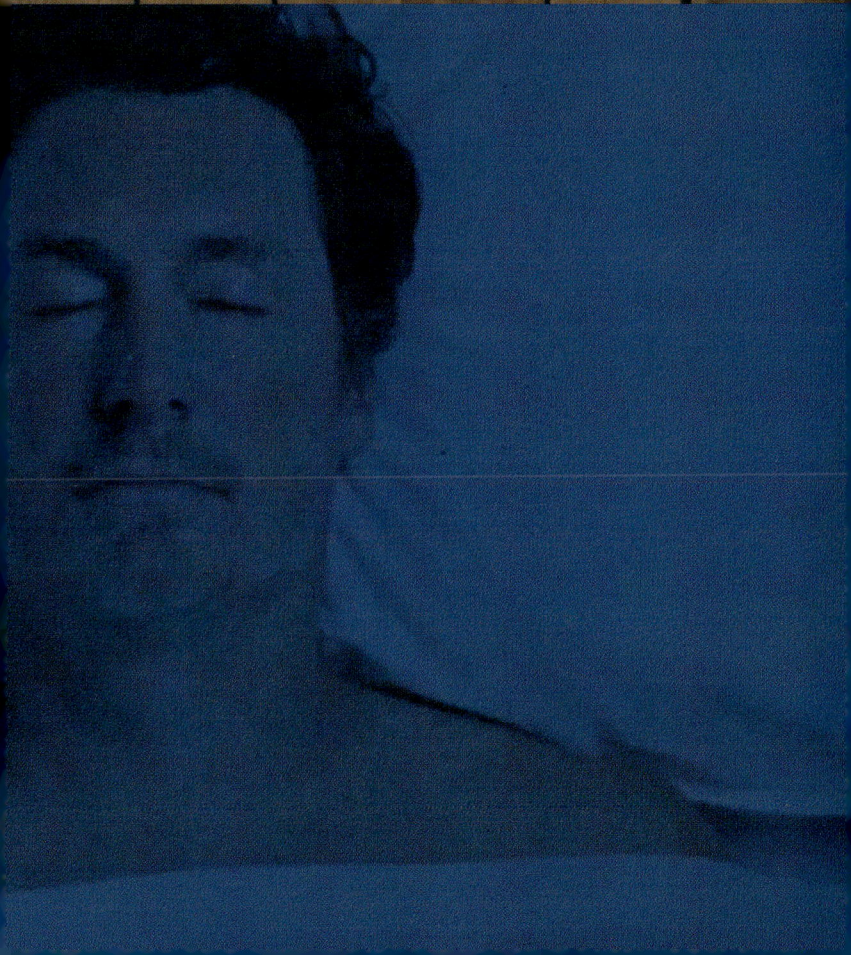

That I'll perform

for a small minority stake from Highland Capital Partners, a Europe-based venture capital firm. The tone of the negotiations felt immediately different than their previous trips to London and Silicon Valley.

The investment group might have not exactly understood all of this brand-building ambition, but they got that it had contributed to year-on-year growth, profitability and a lot of loyalty among the user base. The millions invested went mostly toward settling the accounts of founders and the people who'd taken tiny salaries from the beginning.

It's interesting to think about what they would've been able to do with a marketing budget the size of Uber, or Nike. If they would have splashed some of the cash on big names and events. Maybe we would have heard more about the brand.

Squarespace took this route. The college developer who founded it in 2003 built it as a design-driven business focused on making website creation easier, and more stylish[3].

The company has taken five rounds of venture funding, most recently in 2021, when they raised $300 million at a $10 billion valuation. It was the same year it debuted on the New York Stock Exchange. Along the way, it has not just defended its space in a competitive market, but shown brand differentiation with unique creative collaborations and memorable Super Bowl ads.

But what would WeTransfer have sacrificed in taking that course?

The company would be quick to say the kind of steady growth that felt manageable, even if that meant founders who were still working day jobs to pay the bills for the first few years.

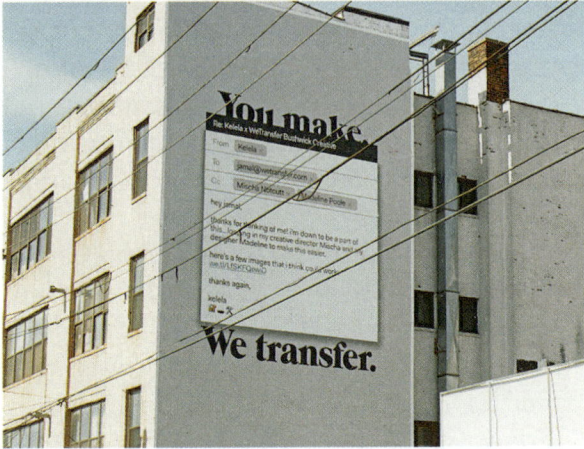

When musician Kelela didn't come up with the promised ad creative in time, WeTransfer used the email exchange between her and the brand instead. The message: creativity is a process.

And though well-funded marketing campaigns might have broadened the customer base, WeTransfer would've missed out on deepening its relationship with the small agencies, solo creatives, musicians and filmmakers who had been using it since day one (and continue to).

Most importantly, though, the team would have missed out on the innovative thinking that comes when money is tight, and the unique culture that produces.

In an environment where big ideas are encouraged, but resources are limited, the team members come to see each euro spent as their own. The constraints—somewhat conversely—encourage bigger, more outlandish thinking.

The teams lean on craft, humor and passion in executing them. Lacking funds for big media buys, they look to create value for creative collaborators through other means, like wallpaper takeovers, or strategically purchased billboards in Brooklyn or downtown LA.

A culture known for empowering this type of creativity also becomes an attractive place to work.

> WeTransfer's 30 percent strategy ended up attracting a lot of talent keen to work for a company that placed so much value in the creative community. Many came from it.

WeTransfer welcomed people from disparate professional backgrounds into its brand and marketing teams, and gave them loosely defined roles. This had a surprising effect on team dynamics.

"Ideas that will get us fired"

and other cultural values.

No one too defined by their job title, or accustomed to working a certain way, was going to take risks. But someone who, like the artists the brand loved, saw themselves as a multivert, might. At the very least they'd slip more comfortably into the role of inquisitive outsider rather than an expert proposing tried-and-true recommendations.

This created a culture of fearlessness, or what I think of as faith. Anybody could present an idea that was meaningful or addressing a need in the creative community from which they came. WeTransfer brand leadership regularly challenged their team and brand creative partners to "come up with ideas that will get us fired."

The resulting campaigns were never predictable, but felt coherent in the brand's narrative: An homage to Carl Sagan and NASA's Golden Record on the 40th anniversary of its launch into space that involved 40 collaborators from 20 countries; the podcast and TikTok series "Drop School," featuring an unknown designer in East London trying to build his one-man fashion brand.

As the company grew, the ideas got more expensive and required more justification. But WeTransfer maintained a simple framework for generating them.

Actually, that's not quite right. They never verbalized this. They definitely didn't print it out, frame it and hang it in conference rooms.

But in talking to the WeTransfer teams past and present about the unique environment that sprouted off-the-wall ideas, their answers felt like a framework of sorts. I pulled them together here.

Start from somewhere else.
Value passion.
Don't disagree and commit,
debate and persuade.
Empower and have faith.

The first is about reframing the context so that people feel encouraged to share unconventional ideas. The second takes into account the belief and energy behind an idea. The third—vital in a small team—is about getting everyone to pull in the same direction. And the fourth is the hardest for most leaders, but the most rewarding for those they lead.

In the 15 years since its founding, WeTransfer has employed hundreds of people. New product features have been introduced, a few new CEOs as well. And yet the framework that ensured a culture that generated—and acted on—meaningful ideas remained the same, even with new layers added on. This ensured not just the product, but the brand itself could enjoy continuity.

It also ensured that reputations and relationships developed early on would enjoy the time needed to flower into something meaningful— such as creative projects with elusive musicians.

In July 2024, SAULT's producer and creator, Inflo, released "Acts of Faith" as one 32-minute track split into separate songs via a WeTransfer link. The response from critics was almost universal in its praise. WeTransfer is still waiting for the film.

PHOTOGRAPHER
TIM WALKER ON FAITH

Why is it important to have faith in what you're creating?

When you're creating you have to have an internal compass. An innate, inherent thing that I'll call a passion-o-meter—a meter that measures when you really believe in something. Something has to feel right to you, whatever that unknown thing is, in order for you to share it with others. It's about having such a keenness to bring that thing you see inside your imagination out into the world that you somehow make it true.

Once you have conviction in your vision, how do you get your creative collaborators on board with it?

Once you've seen something in your daydreams... the power of the desire to show it to others is what moves people to work alongside you. You have to utterly believe in your vision in order to get everyone to run the distance with you.

105

INSTINCT

Use data to identify
opportunities.

Use instinct to build
an identity that resonates with
your community.

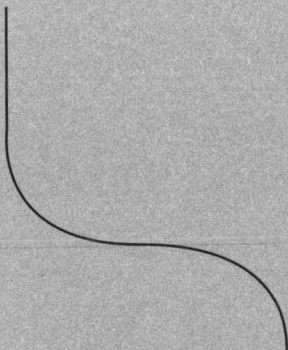

Then take bigger risks
to grow.

You're nearing the end of this book so you know
by now that WeTransfer decided from the outset
not to collect masses of user data. This was
anathema to the way internet businesses were
built (and still is). User data has led to trillion
dollar companies helmed by our world's most
idiosyncratic and influential moguls (see:
Zuckerberg, Mark, or Bezos, Jeff). It's also led to
an incredibly generic internet.

There's no doubt WeTransfer would have
been able to serve itself and its advertising clients
better with more specific information around its
user base. Instead, it opted for a light data relationship with those who visited WeTransfer, even
after starting a "pro" level subscription in 2012.
This meant WeTransfer never "owned" its audience in the way other companies did.

We know, of course, that entire businesses
were built on targeting data in the direct-to-con-
sumer social media age that turned companies
into brand names very quickly. Some have stayed,
others have faded from memory. All balance on
a knife's edge.

They must satisfy investor goals while con-
fronting the rising cost of reaching customers on
the very social platforms that enabled them to
build their business.

They also face the growing dis-
comfort we have with the level

of information companies pos-
sess and the ease with which
we're targeted.

And yet data is so important to a brand.
The right information on your desired customers
informs not just the products you might develop,
or how you launch a marketing campaign, but to
whom, where and when. What the data doesn't
provide is Why.

That's because Why is further upstream,
informed by the narrative the brand has created
around itself in the marketplace. Sometimes this
is overtly mission-driven, like Stella McCartney's
founding story as a force for sustainability in
fashion, but it doesn't always have to be. It can
be as simple as wanting to create a sleek way
to share files with minimum fuss, and providing
a platform to the creatives who use it.

Data-poor compared to its competitors in
the 2010s, WeTransfer worked entirely on instinct
when building its narrative. In fact, in talking to
those who were building the brand at the time,
not one seemed to have a detailed idea of who,
exactly, the WeTransfer audience was until
around 2017, when the company began hiring
traditional marketing and insights roles.

This was risky, but also freeing. Decisions
were made on taste and point of view, not market
segments. Healthy debates were had at lunch

Data-poor,

rich
in instincts.

over a sought-after artist's latest album, and whether it disqualified them from a possible collaboration.

> When talking about their audience, they avoided using the term "users," with its weird suggestion of drug addiction, and looked at ways they could deepen the relationship with the people coming to the platform.

When featuring artists on WePresent, the team sometimes created surprise giveaways and content, such as downloadable posters and music. There was so much obsession with being different and new that the young company often pivoted quickly, and unnecessarily. There was a lot of expended energy as the brand zigged between the right artist and the right moment, trying to anticipate culture.

Eventually, the team formed a consensus on the type of creatives WeTransfer coveted: multi-hyphenates who were fearless in the mediums they explored and the issues they tackled therein. One founder often referred to the impossible-to-pin-down John Malkovich as a model.

As the company grew and more traditional marketing and insights roles were added in the late 2010s, the team worked smarter to

"AMERICAN"
with Robin de Puy

Created between 2022 and 2024, "AMERICAN" is a collection of audio, video and still portraits by Dutch photographer Robin de Puy. WePresent released the project less than three weeks after the United States voted in Donald Trump for a second term. De Puy's portraits focused on everyday Americans she met on her travels through the country. The team built a microsite for the work with 25 episodes, the last nine captured in the summer of 2024.

understand the WeTransfer audience and what resonated. When they saw that photographers made up the largest group of paid subscribers, they doubled down on commissioning photo projects, creating guides and setting up photography events.

As more musicians and groups worked, in the last couple of years, to reclaim the direct relationships with their fans that streaming and ticketing services had monopolized, WeTransfer built tools to make it easier for them.

In 2023, the dance group Jungle approached the brand, looking for someone to finance their music video. WeTransfer instead created a global campaign around their new album, with a release cadence set in coordination with the company's marketing team.

It included album art downloads, a behind-the-scenes zine and interactive wallpaper. The campaign saw big increases to monthly active users on WeTransfer, as well as an increase in account sign-ups.

But the company also understood the limits of the insights and data it was collecting. The user surveys the brand commissioned showed its group was highly-educated, health-conscious, climate-change aware and possessed a certain degree of affluence[4]. That was very useful in appealing to the top luxury brands that advertised on the platform, but less helpful in

Decisions made on taste,

not

market segments.

informing who to collaborate with in brand campaigns, or what storytelling got the green light.

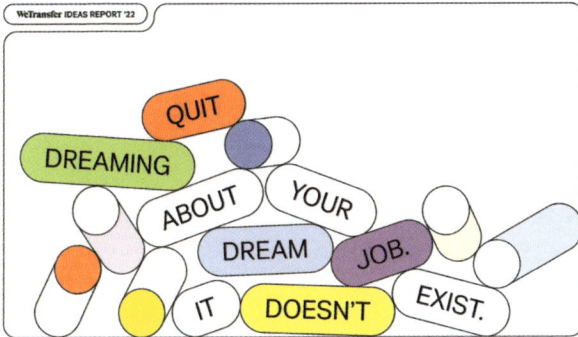

WeTransfer IDEAS REPORT '22

QUIT DREAMING ABOUT YOUR DREAM JOB. IT DOESN'T EXIST.

The Ideas Reports surveyed tens of thousands of the file-sharing service's user base. Each report—five in all—focused on different themes, from motivation to process and the massive shifts the creative industry continues to undergo.

Plus, like all hard data, it was backwards-looking. It couldn't definitively predict what might come next. What could, in certain respects, was WePresent's brand storytelling, which offered the sort of qualitative research for which most companies turn to outside agencies. Sure, the articles, podcast series, film projects and videos drove new users to WeTransfer and converted some existing ones to subscriptions.

But the work was also serving a bigger purpose: the brand was uncovering what it meant to be

a working creative in a rapid-
ly-changing world, and positioning
WeTransfer as both their advocate and source of inspiration.

That WeTransfer was able to do this speaks to
the fact that it had a fully fledged personality,
built largely on the instincts of the people
that worked there. They treated the audience
the way they wanted to be treated themselves:
with respect, trust and dollops of inspiration.
The brand-first approach kept WeTransfer top
of mind, which made the SEO and the email
marketing work better.

From 2018 to 2020, the company enjoyed
a compound annual growth rate of 31 percent, on
the back of double-digit percentage increases in
its revenue, made up of subscriptions and advertising[5]. WeTransfer was readying itself for an IPO
on the Amsterdam Stock Exchange at this point,
keen to pay off that private equity investment
from 2015 and develop the brand and product for
new audiences.

Though volatile markets doomed the plan,
the leadership still saw opportunities to take
advantage of a growing movement of creators,
many new to the game, who needed collaborative
tools that were simple and straightforward.

The storytelling upheld the brand narrative
of creative facilitation to this new addressable

market. WePresent unveiled annual Ideas Reports, based on interviews with its audience that investigated changes and challenges in the creative and creator industry. It published guides for photographers, videographers and illustrators looking to start or level up their business.

All the while, it continued to curate the curators. And the creatives it partnered with enticed other, bigger collaborations.

That's how a partnership with Cynthia Shanmugalingam turned into a film with Riz Ahmed.

ACTOR RUSSELL TOVEY
ON INSTINCT

Does instinct play a role in your creative process?

Instinct is a very important energy that I trust and have gratitude for in myself. I see myself as an instinctive actor—meaning I am open to the opportunity of improv, to chance and accident, to being the vessel for reacting to the first thought that comes to you. The first inclination. The instinct. It's like an ingrained notion, and a real leap of faith and trust in your own thoughts and feelings when you're an artist.

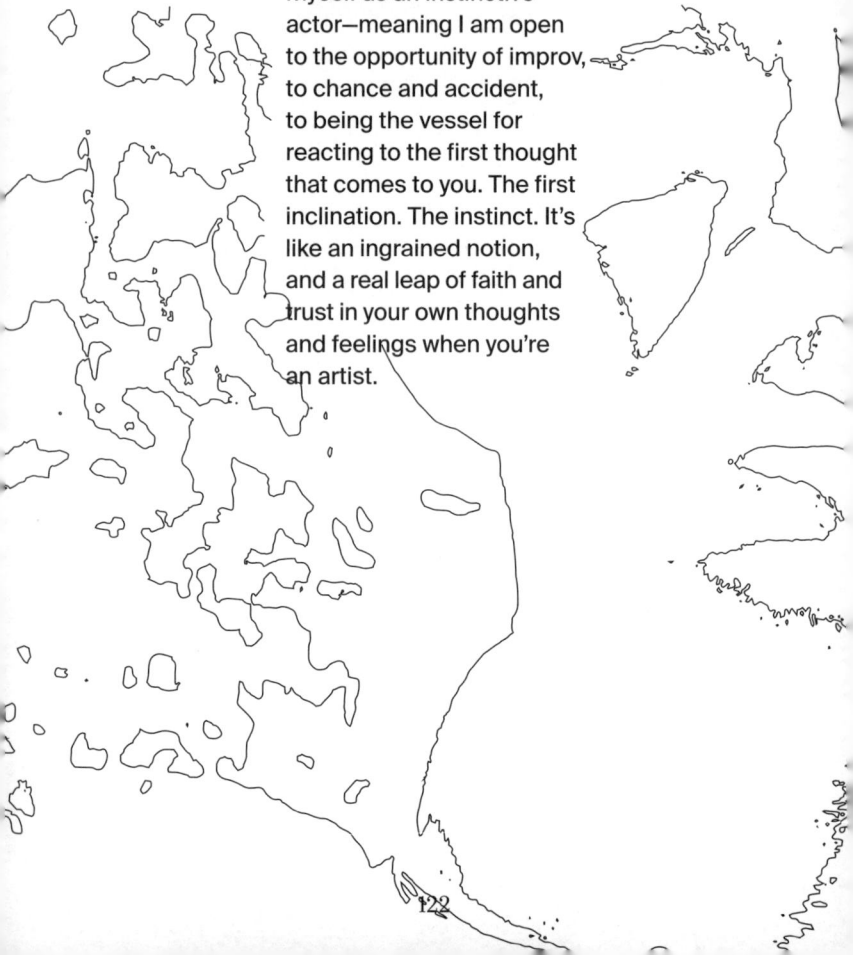

Instinct

Do you see differences in approach, though, when it comes to creating art?

So in acting, I think there's instinctive actors and technical actors. Technical actors like to know where they're standing, what line they're saying at what point, how they're going to react, how the other person is going to give their line to them, how they're going to respond. Whereas instinctive actors—who I find the most exciting and who I consider myself as—are actors that can change things up all the time, react in a different way, go with it, and be in the moment. Instinctive-ness in art is basically being in the moment.

When it comes to a visual artist, when you look at artists who are abstract expressionists, that is all about instinct, that's all about going with where the paint is pushing you, where the brush is taking you, where your body wants to go. It's improvising on a surface. Instinct really plays into expressionism more. Because it's how one thing makes you react and move the narrative, move the story forwards. Instincts, basically, propel us as storytellers into new opportunities.

SERENDIPITY

There is luck, ———————— and there
is serendipity,

which needs to
be cultivated.

Create the conditions for it

by working with the right
intention, trust, faith and
instincts in the community
you've built.

At the very beginning of WeTransfer, when companies weren't buying ads, two of the founders traveled from Amsterdam to London at least twice a month. They'd look up companies they thought might be interested in a premium advertising environment, and knock on their doors (or charm their building receptionists) to try and get meetings.

After one failed attempt, they walked past a building in Shoreditch with a small sign that read "It's Nice That." The design website for young creatives was based in the British capital, but the two founders couldn't really believe that they'd happened upon the It's Nice That office. They rang the buzzer.

Within minutes, they were welcomed not just into the office, but the warm embrace of a community of It's Nice That employees who not only knew WeTransfer, but were slightly in awe that its founders had knocked on their door.

> The product, as it were, had found its community. In real life.

Far more than any business opportunity (though WeTransfer would sponsor It's Nice That's creative conference series) the meeting made the two tired founders realize their brand was resonating with the audience they were building for all along.

This wasn't luck; this was serendipity. The groundwork had been laid by the effort they put in and the many rejections they'd experienced. What landed in their laps that day was a small acknowledgment from the universe for all of their efforts.

Brands have been built on less. Play-Doh was a wallpaper cleaner before a teacher saw her kids playing with it as a modeling compound and a global hit was born. Slack started life as an internal comms tool for a tech company building an entirely different product[6]. It was only when that failed, that the founders realized what was hiding in plain sight and created another way for the corporate world to communicate (oh, goody).

The path to Oscar-winning films, it turns out, is paved with many moments of serendipity. In WeTransfer's case, it began with a British-Sri Lankan chef. Cynthia Shanmugalingam was a friend of an occasional WeTransfer production partner. She was in the process of opening a new restaurant in London and wanted to travel to Sri Lanka—small camera team in tow—on the search for unique ingredients and recipes.

WeTransfer agreed to the small budget and placed the resulting 3 minute and 45 second short on WePresent, a charming, simple collaboration that didn't get them any press or major traffic hits.

At an event a few weeks later, Shanmugalingam spoke about that film to Riz Ahmed's
manager, Caroline Reason. Reason sent an email
to WePresent looking for some financial support
and distribution for a project her client was
working on.

The editor emailed back, and after sev-
eral months of email chains and brainstorming
calls, WePresent received Ahmed's treatment,
which focused on his fear of rising racism and
hate crimes after Great Britain voted to leave
the European Union. An equally skilled musician, Ahmed had planned a new album around
the idea, called "The Long Goodbye." The film,
directed by Aneil Karia, was deeply personal and
meant to serve as the visual accompaniment to
the album.

It was filmed on the two shortest days of
the year in 2019, close to Christmas. In early
February, WeTransfer received the first edit.
In 11 tight, sobering minutes, Karia and Ahmed
unfurled a taut drama in post-Brexit Britain
where paramilitary forces rounded up South
Asian Britons from their homes, wreaking chaos
and bloodshed.

The brand had taken a political stance
before. WeTransfer took action within a week
of the Parkland high school shooting in Florida
in 2018, for example. It didn't just produce a short
film by military veterans calling for the ban of

Dare the universe, and it might dare you back.

assault rifles like the type used in the shooting,
but suspended advertising on its platform for
an entire weekend to promote it. The film was
played during the March for Our Lives rally in
Washington, DC. WePresent also commissioned
seven artists to create posters that people could
print to use at protests.

That event prompted the company to
develop a set of guidelines that determined how,
exactly, it would participate in political topics.

> It wouldn't issue statements,
> or attach itself to every cause.
> Rather, it would speak through
> the artists it featured, offering
> up its platform and reach.

But this film felt like a bigger risk. In its history of
promoting the arts, the brand had exposed itself
to pushback from users for controversial content
more than a few times. There was a good chance
"The Long Goodbye," with its violent scenes and
harsh critique of racism and Brexit, could inflame
discussion. Plus, it's not an easy watch, and most
of the WeTransfer audience used the product
during working hours.

The film made its debut on WeTransfer on
March 6, 2020, just a week before COVID-19 shut
down the world. The London-based production
company Somesuch, which had co-produced

the film, and WeTransfer submitted the film to
festivals, and it began winning—first, for Best UK
Short at Raindance in 2020, then Best British
Short Film at the British Independent Film
Awards the same year. When it won the Grand
Prix at the Odense International Film Festival in
2021, it officially qualified for the Oscars.

In early February 2022, almost two years
after it debuted on WePresent, the team watched
the Oscar nominations on YouTube separately.
When "The Long Goodbye" made the short list,
the group exchanged a flurry of excited texts.

At a party arranged by the brand in
the Hollywood Hills the night before the Oscars
ceremony, Ahmed got up to speak. What he said
about WeTransfer went beyond an acknowledgement of financing and distribution. In many ways,
it validated the brand's foundation of trust.

And though someone captured it in
an iPhone video, there was no attempt by
the company to capitalize on these beautiful
words, by, say, creating a marketing campaign around it. How very WeTransfer. They'll
never learn.

Here, a condensed version:

"What a beautiful, pleasant surprise
this has been. You guys have really
revolutionized and enabled artists to
be able to communicate and connect

with one another in what you do on your platform. And this I see as just an extension to that, and amplification of that.

You connected us to our true artistic voice. Because it is very rare that you are given the support and the carte blanche to go and just find your voice. Not even like, 'Yo, we'd love it if you could get a laptop in there, sending some MP3s across.'

I remember when we put this treatment together, we said, 'We'll say this, this is what we want to do, but don't worry, they'll never let us make that.' And we were almost daring the universe.

The most you can hope for from a creative partner, from a patron, from people trying to enable you, is to dare you back. And that's what you did. You said, 'You want to make that? Make it.'"

In his excellent book on intuition, "Thinking, Fast and Slow," the late Daniel Kahneman wrote about narrative fallacy; the concept (first introduced

by essayist and statistician Nassim Taleb) refers
to our mind's tendency to construct easily
accessible, overconfident judgements in order to
make sense of unexpected success (or failure).
In these narratives, said Kahneman, we assign
a larger role to talent, stupidity and intentions
than to luck[7].

So it's important to state the enormous
degree of luck WeTransfer experienced in winning an Oscar.

There were a series of small decisions and
events that happened to lead to the Great Big
Thing: the right creative partner; the buzz around
the emerging star who made it; the found budget
for the Oscar PR campaign that found its mark.

So much of brand-building is about making
the right decisions at the right moments, with
little more than the information available to you
at the time. Even then, it actually just comes
down to groups of people and leaders with
a clear vision.

In WeTransfer's case, that vision was to set
beautiful and powerful creative projects out in
the world with the hope that they resonated.

That the team had the audience to whom
that sort of mission appealed helps explain
WeTransfer's growth and success as a business over the last 15 years. If they had behaved
as a typical enterprise software company they
would've had to lose the simplicity and freedom

"The Long Goodbye"
with Aneil Karia and Riz Ahmed

Filmed over the two shortest days of the year in 2019, the journey from the film's debut on WeTransfer on March 6, 2020 to the Oscars two years later involved heavy campaigning by WePresent editor Holly Fraser, co-producers Somesuch Productions and Ahmed's manager. "Let's just get to nomination phase," Fraser remembers

thinking. "Anything else is a bonus." Since the Oscar win, the brand has seen a flood of high quality idea submissions. "The Brown Dog," a short WeTransfer produced in 2024, featuring Steve Buscemi and the voice of the late actor Michael K. Williams, qualified for the Animated Shorts category at the 2025 Oscars.

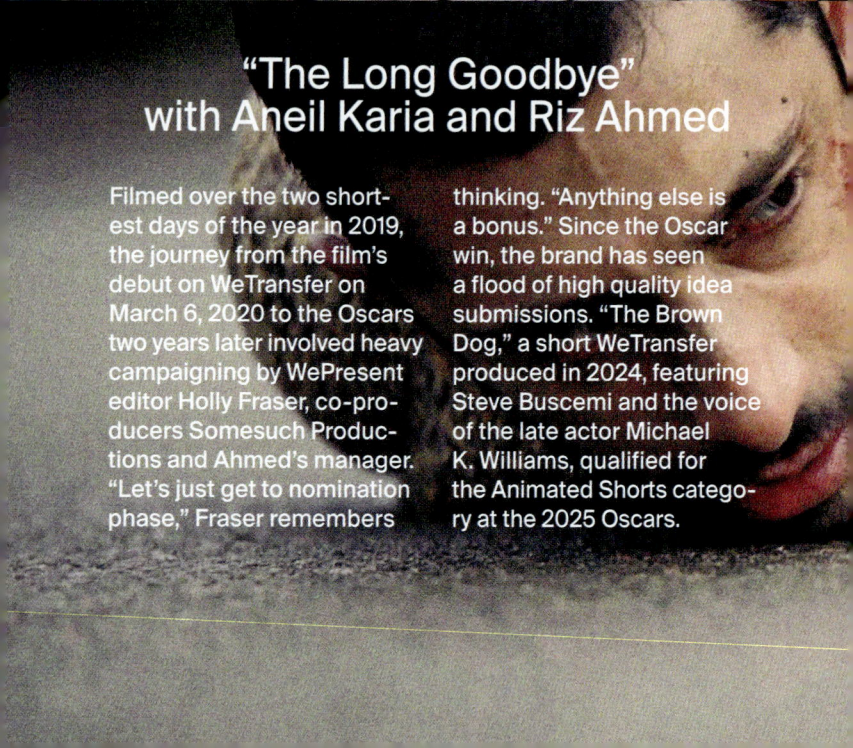

in favor of security, a strategy that would've lost core fans in an effort to gain large corporate clients. If they had relied purely on performance marketing to build their customer base, they might have entered a price race that put them out of existence.

Maybe this is the path the company will take now. A few months after we started working on this book, WeTransfer was acquired. In the second week of September 2024, the new owners announced plans to make 75 percent of the company's employees redundant[8]. Included were most of the leaders who built and sustained the creative brand.

The vision for the future is unclear, but one the new owners have described as a smaller, more focused WeTransfer. You can imagine them stopping just short of writing "back to basics."

But that's just it. The basics of WeTransfer have always been about a commitment to empowering creativity and humanity through a product founded on trust. What comes next is not a return to that, but a new chapter—applauded and encouraged by investors with an appetite for profit, growth, maybe even the IPO that proved so elusive.

And they might want to pave the way not with values like intention, trust, faith, instinct and serendipity, but hard data, reduced costs and predictable outcomes.

The mission and merits of lower case b brands.

What remains independent is the Supporting Act Foundation, which is somehow fitting. Providing no-strings-attached €10,000 to €50,000 grants to artists and nonprofit organizations, the Supporting Act represents the purest form of the WeTransfer ethos. Its core values are identical to those that WeTransfer held as it built its brand.

WePresent, as well, will continue to surprise and delight with storytelling and creative collaborations that seek to push cultural conversation forward.

Their existence ensures a continued role for WeTransfer in the creative community it helped support. And maybe this book, and the ideas that turned a Dutch file-sharing company into a globally recognized brand, provide the seeds for someone else.

The timing feels right.

Social media companies and Google have revealed themselves as untrustworthy partners in helping companies build audiences. More brands are shifting budgets away from them, keen to find more effective ways to build relationships with the people they want to reach.

The VC environment is no longer as delirious as in the past decade, with investors shying away from big bets on startups (without "AI" high up in their pitch decks) at a steady rate since 2021[9]. A more patient approach forces open a lane for the kind of slower, manageable growth that benefits long-term brand-building the most.

And though the climate catastrophe may be ringing alarm bells, it's also spurring the creation of thousands of businesses that recognize their brand differentiation is in both their innovative products and the intention with which they're built.

Those conditions still require actions by companies that run counter to the status quo. Most will aspire to be capital B brands, looking to maximize their reach quickly by appealing to as many audiences as possible, and claim market share with high-risk, high-reward campaigns and collaborations.

But for others, there's another, equally rewarding path: one that sees users and customers as a community to start a conversation with, build with and, eventually, partner with. Those companies are the ones that will walk before they run, bring their audience along with them as they grow, and believe a list of values only work when they're put into action.

That might turn them into brands that dominate our headspace, or it might turn them into lower case b brands that resonate in a more subtle, meaningful way. Brands that exist to add value to a community of like-minded people. Brands like WeTransfer.

END NOTES

1   WeTransfer data sourced from company releases
2   "Let My People Go Surfing" by Yvon Chouinard, Penguin
     Books, 2005
3   "Why Would Anyone Make a Web Site in 2023?
     Squarespace CEO Anthony Casalena Has Some Ideas,"
     Decoder podcast, 18/7/2023
4   WeTransfer internal customer insights report,
     February 2024
5   Creativity Productivity Group Prospectus, January 2022
6   "Slack and Flickr: Stewart Butterfield," How I Built
     This podcast, 30/7/2018
7   "Thinking, Fast and Slow" by Daniel Kahneman,
     Penguin Books, 2011
8   "Bending Spoons plans to lay off 75% of WeTransfer
     staff after acquisition" Tech Crunch, 8/9/2024
9   "Global private equity and venture capital entries
     worldwide since 2019," S&P Global

A big thank you to researcher and editor
Alice Sweitzer, as well as current and former
WeTransfer employees whose insight was invalu-
able in constructing this narrative.

Rob Alderson
Danielle Boelling
Keith Butters
Stephen Canfield
Michael Fitzsimmons
Holly Fraser
Tara Goutermout
Nessim Higson
Jenne Meerman
Lukas Nieuwenhuijsen
Ciara O'Shea
Thijs Remie
Lina Ruiz
Annematt Ruseler
Tiffany Yu

And to all WeTransfer teams
past and present.

Wassila Abboud, Jenna Abrams, Irene Achterbergh, Arenike Adebajo, Inès
Aguinaga, Mirella Agyemann, Oluwaseni Ajamajebi, Farhan Ajram, Mark
Ajram, Oluwafemi Akinde, Mohamad Alasrawi, Diana Alcausin, Robert
Alderson, Lalith Allaka, Andrew Allen, David Allen-Jordan, Allyssia Alleyne,
Luana Almeida, Marta Alterio, Alex Alves, Julian Alves, Fabienne
Amirkhan, Sebastian Ammon, Irena Ljubikj Ampova, Julia Andrzejewska,
Asya Angelova, Christina Apao, João Apolinario, Mohammadreza Arabi,
Yonnas Araya, Constantina Archeou, Veronica Arghinenti, Yenderly
Coromoto Hernandez Aristigueta, Andrii Arkhipov, Ana Arlamenko,
Mathieu Artu, Rohini Aru, Arman Arutiunov, Michael Avishay, Ilia
Awakimjan, Stephen Awolaja, Gemma Aylward, Nathan Azoti-Wright,
Khatchik Bagdassarian, Kees Bakker, Raj Balaiyan, Kim Ballemans,
Akanksha Bansal, Bogdan Banu, Rochelle Baptiste-Peter, Rafael Ramos
Regis Barbosa, Taylor Barnhill, Jo-Anne Barrow, Dmytro Basiuk, Erica
Baskin, Diogo Batista, Stefanie Bazarian, Steven Bazarian, Alberto
Becerra, Nathan Beck, Mirte Becker, Stephanie Beech, Samuel Beek, Bas
Beerens, Lan Belic, Devin Beliveau, Andrew Bell, Samad Bellafkih, Ilaria
Bellanca, Fabien Bellini, Brent Benadè, Allyson Benas, Roos van den Berg,
Stacy Bergener, Birthe Emma Marrij Bergs, Noah Berman, Sofia
Bernardo, Beau Bertens, Jana Bertram, Malvika Bhatnagar, Alexa Biale,
Tom Biddulph, Reinier Bierkens, Oleksandr Bilochenko, Tom Bird, Karin
Biseswar, Vera le Blanc, Alix Blankson, Claudio Di Blasi, Berit Block, Bob
Blom, Arjen van Bochoven, Danielle Boelling, Slobodan Bogdanovic, Harry
De Bok, Sarah Bondoc, Alex Bonilla, David Boot, David Bosveld, Arthur
Botha, Toby Bourne, Anne Bowerman, Sebass Gerardus Matheus van
Boxel, Méadhbh Boyle, Rob Cornelis Petrus van Bogaard den Braaf,
Damian John Bradfield, Kirsty Bradley, Peter Bradley, Jason Bradley, Pete
Brady, Andrew Braini, Marc Bramaud, Nathalie Brandt, Maud Bressers,
Evgeni Britanov, Bas Broek, Isabella Brookes, Brad Brooks, Liam Brosnan,
Travis Brown, Marvin de Bruin, Janna Brummel, Emma Bruns, Francesco
Bruzzo, Rachel Buchholtzer, Natasha Bukholt, Daniel Buoro-Ejimade,
Gwendolyn Burbidge, Luca Burgio, Brandi Burgus, Jet van den Busken,
Polly Bussell, Samantha Butters, Keith Butters, Matthew Butts, Rey
Caacbay, April Cain, Tylar Calcinai, Josh Caley-Brown, Haja Camara, Aidan
Cammell, Andrea Cammi, Muhammet Can, Stephen Canfield, Amy Cao,
Davide Carletti, Vinícius Magalhães do Carmo, Alyssa Carrasco, John
Carrick, Jack Carrick, Roberta Carta, Troy Carter, Gabriela Carvalho,
Michael Casalaina, Federica Castagnetti, Valerio Castelli, Omer Celik,
Daniel Hernandez Chacon, Heather Champ, Natascha Chamuleau, Julie
Chamuleau, Leonora Chance, Awantika Chand, Cece Chandra,
Chuphangini Chandrakanthan, Jeremiah Chaney, Nikki Chapman,
Meredith Chapman, Arnaud Charpentier, Fidelity Chauke, Terri Chen,
Howard Chen, Maryna Chervinska, Alexander Chia, Leonardo Chiappalupi,

Risa Chik, Kat Chilton, Catalina Chiorbeaca, Ciara Choi, Unathi Chonco, James Christie, Solomiia Chukivska-Marichko, KJ Chun, Donovan Clarke, Angus Clayton, Duarte Sancho Cândido, Emma Coker, Beatrice Colli, Robyn Collinge, Amie Colosa, Dan Conti, Raul Martinez Conzalez, Peter Coolen, Brandon Copeman, Hannah Corbett, Francesco Costantini, Andrew Cowan, Sara Goberna Crespo, Alban Creton, Pablo Crivella, Kaia Crowe, Tyler Cruz, Maximiliano Céspedes, Andjelka Cubrakovic, Matthew Cullerton, Danielle Cummins, Azita Daddeh, Simon Dagfinrud, Clete Ronald Dalid, Flora Dalton, Ivan Danci, Matteo Danieli, Lily Darby, Clara Vanni D'Archirafi, Ignacio Darras, Dhimanjyoti Das, Muhammad Daud, Jamal Dauda, Sam Dave, Gillian Davis, India Davis, Fatema Dawoodbhoy, Mark Dawson, Damon Dean, Sophie Ginoux Defermon, Vivian Dehning, Alex Delbono, Franjoli Deleon, Davide Delucchi, Annematt Ruseler, Mandy Derks, Pierre Allavène d'Erlon, Christa Deslauriers, Kaira Diagne, Leonidas Diamantis, Alessandro Diano, Irina Dima, Alexandre Dobis, Eva Dominaite, Tobia Donati, Filippo Donisi, Bridget Dooley, Olivier Doornink, Arina Doroshenko, Joel van Dorp, John Douglas, Nicholas Dowse, Amy Doyle, Alina Dracopol, Floris van Driel, Helene van den Dries, Giulian Drimba, Rick Dronkers, Benjamin Dryden, Carlos Duchicela, Milena Dudic, Laura Duglio, Jurriaan Marinus Nicolaas Duivenvoorden, Jonathan Dul, Sherilyn Dunk, Anna Dvorak, April Edgar, Faye Ehrich, Merlijn Leonhard Christiaan van Eijk, Fleur Ellis, Boris Emorine, Rene Engelbrecht, Luuk Engele, Titus Engels, Rupert Englander, Michael Enriquez, Marina Erlikh, Claudio Erriu, Jennifer Escotto, Claire Eskandari, Sofia Evans, Colette Sloet tot Everlo, Stijn Eversdijk, Hannah Ewens, Rhianna Exall, Lennart Den Exter, Tim Faber, Icaro Seara Fahning, Ian Fairbrother, Marc Farnworth, Rabbie Faruque, Pietro Fazzini, Tara Feener, Racquel Fenton, Luca Ferrari, Orlando Ferreiro, Lara Ferro, Giovanni Filaferro, Ivamacio Magalhães Filho, Natalie Fisher-Brown, Michael Fitzsimmons, Arno Fleming, Lucie de Lamorte Félines, Milou Foole, Niccolò Foralli, David Forsey, Ashley Fowler, Larry Fox, Martha Lane Fox, Daniel França, Angelina Franchuk, Irina Franghiu, Phie Franse, Holly Fraser, Sarah Fretwell, Valerie Fuchs, Kayleigh Fugatt, Helen Fung, Hope Furniss, Barbara Galiza, Ornella Gallo, Tim Gardner, Nicolas Garnier, Arkaitz Garro, Veronica Garza, Anna Gaspar, Dominic Geargeoura, Dan Gee, Domenico Gemoli, Fatma Genc, Anita Gerding, Alberto Germano, Camilla Gerosa, Pratik Ghedia, Rachel Ghurahoo, Francesco Giacchè, Lee Gibson, Silja Giudici, Daniel Gogov, Irena Goldenberg, Alejandro Perez Gonzalez, Raúl Martinez Gonzalez, Juan Gonzalez-Vallinas, Tom Gordon, Tom Goulooze, Tara Goutermout, Julia Grandfield, Lorenzo Grandi, Maedhbh Greene, Everton Guilherme, Britta Hallebo, Saskia Hamilton, Anita Hammer, Emese Hamza, Leen Hannoon, Mykola Hapon, Marisa Harary, Gregory Harris, Lucy Harris, Sanne van Hattum, Martina Havrlentova,

Ihor Havrylov, Aya Hayashida, Nelly Ben Hayoun, Mark Healy, Mohammad Heidari, Rodney Heijjer, Melinda Heilman, Grant Heinlein, Lotte van Hemert, Joost Hendrikx, Bryce Henry, Suzanne Hermans, Eduardo Hernandez, Michelle Hersisia, Nessim Higson, Patricia Velasco Hijma, Rebecca Hill, Wander Hillen, Amy Hinchliffe, Nathan Hoang, Scott Holcombe, Marili 't Hooft-Bolle, Sander Hooghiemstra, Andrei Horak, Rajani Hore, Matthew Hoskins, Carly Hubregtse, Thomas Hudson, Lee Hudson, James Huffman, Erik Huggers, Kin Hui-Lo, Joris van Huët, Sandi Huynh, Martin Ingram, Alianna Inzana, Spyridon Ioakeimidis, Spyros Ioakeimidis, Ahmad Izreig, Aline Jansen, Willem Jansen, Sana Javed, Hari Jayapalan, Connor Jednak, Belen Jerez, Jevgenij Jermakov, John Jervis, Kyung Jin, Piers John, Phoebe Johnson, Seth Johnson, Donall Johnston, Florian Jonathans, Jort de Jong, Gosse de Jong, Katia Malashyna-de Jong, Leanne Joseph, Roy Everhardus Wilhelmus Kaats, Ali Kabeel, Maarten Matthijs Kadiks, Alex Kahl, Filip Kalinowski, Navid Kamalzadeh, Yulia Kanapatskaya, Marie Kane, John Kantor, Ioannis Kapsalis, Yiannis Kapsalis, Yannis Karagkiouloglou, Fleuri-Anne Karsten, Vedant Kashyap, Sandeep Kaur, Clare Keaveny, Christopher Keenan, Nathan Keighley, Erin Kelly, Sean Kelly, Willeke Kemkers, Robbie Kerr, Andriy Khlopyk, Amir Khorsandi, Stephen Kiernan, Esther Kim, Katherine Kious, Stephanie Kirk, Sara Eszter Kis, Ivan Kiselev, Gabor Kiss, Pauline Klieber, Collin Klippel, Oksana Kobrynska, Lija Kocergina, Raphael Koebraam, Mathieu Leon Kok, Bea Komolafe, Jorn de Koning, Gerrit-Jan Kooijman, Nienke Koorn, Olga Korchevskaya, Emmalotta Korhonen, Roman Kotyk, Yevhen (Eugene) Kozar, Karen van de Kraats, Bram Krekels, Manfred Krikke, Erik Kroes, Phil van der Krogt, Vanja Krstonijevic, Bohdan Kryvyak, Maksym Kryzhanovskyi, Ankush Kumar, Ravishekar Kumar, Darren Kunar, Pavlyna Kupryk, Sara Kushma, Charlotte Lafferty, Jacky Lai, Ka Chun Lai, Yil Kee Lam, Emilie van der Lande, John Carolus de Lang, Lauren Larsen, Nikita Lastovych, Nicola Latham, Allen Lau, Sebastiaan Laurentius, Xuan Ky Le, Leo Lecuyer, Anna Lee, Chris Lee, Antoine van der Lee, Amanda Leone, David Leseman, Gifford Leung, Qing Li, Shirley Li, Tjing Heng Li, Ilia Liachin, Florence Libbrecht, Max Liberman, Michel Ligtvoet, Bilal Limi, Celia Gomez Limia, James Limon, Jiaxin Lin, Camille Lindbom, Melanie Linehan, Alex Lingeman, Zhiyuan Liu, Teresa Lobos, Lisa Loffredo, Christine Loftus, Emily Logan, Carolina Londoño, Jordy van der Loo, Flávio Lourenço, Casper Lourens, Yvonne Lu, Fabio Luccioletti, Dotte Lucker, Jacob Ludington, Daria Luganskaia, Ruud Luijten, Yannick Luijten, Saga Lundqvist, Natalie Lungu, Hayden Lutek, Tatiana Magdaleno, Mats-Olov Magdesjö, Kassim Maguire, Emil Mahmudzade, Annie Malarkey, Katia Malashyna, Matt Maltby, Sally Mambi, Christian Manasci, Francesco Mancone, Saar Manders, Javier Llorente Mans, Sofia Marchese, Julia Markhadaeva, Rui Marques, Becky Martin, Jack Martin, Kristofer Martin,

Marco Martina, Enrico Martinelli, Kelub Martyr, Lisa Anne van Mast-
bergen, Nicole Masterson, Alex Mattinson, Gianluca Maurina, Alessandro
Mautone, Dean Maw, Callum McCruden, Davy McGeorge, Kevin McGonigle,
Edward McKay, Aline Mecke, Margaret Meehan, Jenne Meerman, Meryem
Meghraoua, Paulo De Melo, Ronen Mendelovitz, Anthony Mendoza, Dennis
Mensen, Maurizio Mento, Linda Mertens, Paul Metsers, Gregory De Meyere,
Ben van Middendorp, Joe Mier, Lorenzo Migliorero, Stefan Mikolajczyk,
Scott Millard, Swaan Miller, Daniel Milton, Ginny Min, Virginia Min, Zaif
Minhas, Jarvis Mishler, Jennyfer Missamou, Claudia Misuriello, Jovche
Mitrejchevski, Adam Mitton, Krishan Modi, Bas Moerland, Anton Moggré,
Shonia Mok, Mara Momcilovic, Brian Monnin, Thomas Montgomery,
Giorgia Morchi, Santiago Suárez Morán, May Moscovitz, Kate Moskowitz,
Allison Moss, Abdul-Raheman Mouhamadsultane, Galih Muhammad,
Haseeb Muhammad, Alexander Mulder, Denis Mulder, Camiel Ignance
Mulders, Hannah Mullen, Thomas Murdoch, Gee Yeol Nahm, Linda
Nakanishi, Dara Nasr, Perry Nauta, Dustin Newbold, Katie Newnham, Vu
Nam Nguyen, Aart Nicolai, Giuseppe Nicoletti, Søren Nielsen, Lukas Peter
Nieuwenhuijssen, Gregory Nimmo, Agathe Niquet, Sheela Nistala, Nitika
Nitika, Cynthia Njuguna, Claire Nooriala, Thomas van Noort, Alexandra
Novikova, Melissa Nussbaum, Sulaiman Obaid, Ciaran O'Brien, Thomas
Offinga, Lucas Oliveira, Carina Oliveira, Wanda Olivier, Evelyn Oluwole,
Tim Van Ommeren, Fin O'Neill, Stevie O'Neill, Stephen O'Neill, Min Ying
Ong, Jochem Oosterveen, Isabella van Oostrom-Schouten, Eveline Oude
Ophuis, Ciara O'Shea, Thirza Ostendorf, Daniela Osterberger, Adam
O'Toole, Amir Ouakri, Marco Pagni, Ulises Soriano Palao, Ricardo de
Castro Palácio, Katrina Pallant, Lumír Španihel, Florinda Pannofino, Ava
Paradise, Xavier Parareda, Brian Park, Oliver Parker, Federico Passa-
lacqua, Francesco Patarnello, Javaad Patel, Vishal Patel, Ragini Patidar,
Sagar Patil, Michele Patrassi, Diandra Patrick, Tessa Pauw, Tommy
Pedrick, Raphaelle Pellerin, BJ Pennington, Beth Pennington, Harry
Peppitt, Ignacio Pereira, Fabio Perella, Maria Perez, Clément Pergaud,
Jarell Perry, Romy Peschar, Isabella Peters, Gilles Peterson, Ruta Peter-
sonaite, Petar Petrovic, Georg Petschnigg, Lauren Phillips, Alan Pich,
Martijn Pieter Bakker, Marco Pietersen, Romain Pietersen, Monika Pijl,
Lucy Victoria Pike, Esteban Pintos, Kata Pintér, Wibo Pipping, Arjan
Polderman, Piotr Politowicz, Radu Popa, Lana Popara, Mihai Popescu, Ilja
Popovs, Hampus Poppius, Marco Porro, James Porteous-Butler, Shannon
Potter, Yugandhar Potti, Esther Pouw, Matteo Pozzetti, Irene Pozzi, Chloe
Precey, Gina Prenger, Matteo Preti, Rebecca Preuss, Kirsty Price, Ish
Prithipal, Keaton Proud, Jaytel Provence, João Prudêncio, Lindsay
Pudavick, Alessio Puddu, Carlo Pulcini, Irina Pulyakhina, Andy Purcell,
Miruna Purice, Alexander Pusey, Zoe Pyle, Faye Quinn, Elisa Ragazzini,
Jonathan Ramos, Silvana Rangel, Nik D Ratcliff, Aditi Rawat, Phoebe

Redlin, Timon Reek, Sam Rees, Silvia Reis, Thijs Remie, Danny Rensen-
brink, Lotte de Reus, Dennis Röhrs, Enrico Ribelli, Sjoerd van Rijen,
Mariska Rijnaarts, Matthew Riley, Bela Rinderu, Fanina Rivai, Robert
Rivellino, Ulrich Rivers, Hugo Stephane Robein, Abbie Robinson, Eric
Rockey, Megan Roderick, Niko Rodriguez, Robert Rodriguez, Brendan
Rogers, Austin Roos, Erika Rossi, Luca de Rosso, Nicolae Rotaru, Liam
Roth-Thomas, Nickie Roudez, Anupama Roy, Denit Rozner, Jacqueline
Ruggiero, Linsey Ruijter, Lina Ruiz, Nina Rutten, Frankie Ryle, Frances
Ryle, Aswathi S, Vidushi Sahni, Tibor Sakota, Filippo Maria De Salazar,
Pato Salazar, Donia Samraoui, Becca Samson, Joey Sanistam, Gabriel
Santiago, Everton Santos, Filippo Sanzani, Chietra Sardjoe, Ali Sattari,
Jennifer Savet, Claudio Scalzo, Davide Scarpazza, David Schagerstrom,
Rogier Scheinck, Marco Schiavone, Eva Scholte, Edwin Schreuder, Thomas
Schrijer, Pablo Perez Schroder, Riccardo Scotti, Gergely Sebestyén, Alexey
Sekachov, Sergei Semenov, Jeffrey Sen, Giacomo Seno, Marika Seo,
Manpreet Singh Sethi, Yara Shammas, Awisa Shamshiri, Dean Shanahan,
Julia Shapiro, John Shapiro, Deva Sharma, Sagar Sharma, Vasily Shelkov,
Adhiti Shetty, Michelle Shewan, Michael Shimchick, Liv Siddall, Onno
Jeroen Siemens, René Sijnke, Mikee Silva, Mikaela Victoria Silva, Raphael
Silva, Federico Simionato, Luca Simonato, Daniel Sinclair, Jatinjumar
Singh, PrabhDeep Singh, Nilesh Sinha, Edward Sit, Nicola Sita, Weronica
Siwiec, Matt Skibiak, Johnny Slack, Rick Fredericus Petrus Theodorus
Smit, Roos Metje Smit, Adam Smith, Eric Smith, Jessica Smith, Shawn
Snyder, Iulia Soare, Donato Solazzo, Themis Chatzi - Sotiriou, Cristiana
Sousa, India van Spall, Massimo Spalla, Lumir Spanihel, Aishwary
Srivastava, Andrea Stano, Nicole Stanton, Christopher Stevens, Kelly
Stevens, Marlouke Stofkooper, Antonije Stojadinovic, Ana Stojic, Olivier
van Straelen, Andreas Strikos, Cyd Stumpel, Shamima Sultana, Andrew
Sulzer, Moniek Suren, Luca Suriano, Aja Sutton, Kirsten Swensen, John
Tan, Nicole Tan, Andrei-Costin Tanasoiu, Pallavi Tandon, Yulian Alek-
seevitch Tarkhanov, Megan Taylor, Mert Tekdemir, Angelique Temple,
Bastiaan Terhorst, Danilo Tesi, Marianna Tessello, Bhargav Thakrar, Triin
Tähema, Joanna Theodorou, Mark Thornton, Federico Tibaldo, Gauke
Tijssen, Hugo Timm, Terezie Štindlová, Elena Tisato, Hitendra Tochia,
Michalis Tolkas, Michail Tolkas, Juraj Toth, Palma Toth, Rissy La Touche,
Holly Townsend, Bernie Trinh, Suzanne Tromp, Alexander Troup, Adriaan
Trouwee, Rebecca Alyssa Trouwee, Lizzie Ttoffali, Aryel Tupinambá,
Noémy Tur, Isabella Fisher Turner, Wojtek Tusz, Danielle Twaalfhoven,
John Twinn, Dmitry Tymchuk, Annemarie van Uden, Audrey Umber, Will
Urmston, Jas Vadgama, Valentina Valdrè, Patricio Valle, Laure Valmier,
Nicholas Vandepeer, Daniela Vandor, Verdiana Vannini, Alexandar Vassilev,
Rik van der Vegte, Alessandro Verardo, Lacey Verhalen, Gerardus Verkerk,
Martijn Vermaat, Marc Vermeeren, Camille Verniolle, Patricio Vidal, Rory

Vigus, Ignatius de Villiers, Razvan Virtan, Maria Vivo, Stafny Vk, Dennis van der Vliet, Ingrid Välk, Heinrich Vogel, Valerio Volpe, Daria Vorontsova, Weyers de Vos, Fatlum Vranovci, Angelo Vreeswijk, Yvo de Vries, Arta Vukaj, Dora Wagner, Irene van der Wal, Jessi Walker, June Wang, Pauline Wang, Saskia Warbout, Isabel Warby, Izzy Ware, Elizabeth Ware, Nicolle Wasserman, Alex Watson, Artur Wdowiarski, Shanelle Weise, Matthew Wells, Amy West, Ruben Westendorp, Gerard Westerhof, Maximiliaan Paulus Franciscus Martinus van Wezel, Keith Whelan, Jasmine Whitaker, Tiger Whiteley, Richard Whitfield, Karlijn van der Wielen, Claudia Wienema, Hugo Wiledal, Alia Wilhelm, Sean Wilkins, Rebecca Williamson, Gordon Willoughby, Matthew Willse, Nilo Van Winden, Sierra Winrow, Daan de Winter, Ruben Wolff, Jeff Wolski, Tammy Wong, Billy Wong, Michael Wood, Sam Woodgate, Jetske van der Wouden, Diane Wrightson, Ezra Xenos, Elif Yagibol-Bal, Moshe Yalovsky, Mark Yalovsky, Mehmet Yaman, Gozde Yildiz, Tiffany Yu, Joseph Yuhas, Shaira Yvel, Figen Zaim, Sara Zaninelli, Tony Zappala, Qining Zeng, James Zepf, Min Zhu, Lucja Zieniewicz, Marleen de Zoete-Kooijmans, Joanna Zoltowska, Laura Zucchinali, Ratidzo Zvirawa, Jansi Zwarts, Sofia Zymnis

A special thanks also to
WeTransfer's founding team
Nalden, Bas Beerens, Rinke Visser, Anne
Zwijnenburg, Dave Forsey and Stefan Verkerk.

KOLOFON***

FUPE Publishing
Amsterdam, the Netherlands

Book design by Kris Pyda, Studio Pyda
Produced by Kris Latocha
Researching and editing by Alice Sweitzer
Proofreading by Esra Gürmen
Art sourcing by Danielle Boelling
Typefaces: GT Super WT, Synt, Suisse Int'l
Printed in Poland

*** (Κολοφών) Definition: Summit, or crowning touch

100[%]

Transferred